Copyright © 2019 Tekkan
Artwork Copyright © 2019

All rights reserved.
First Printing, 2019
ISBN 978-1-7343510-3-3

To contact Tekkan please email:
buddhaboy1289@gmail.com

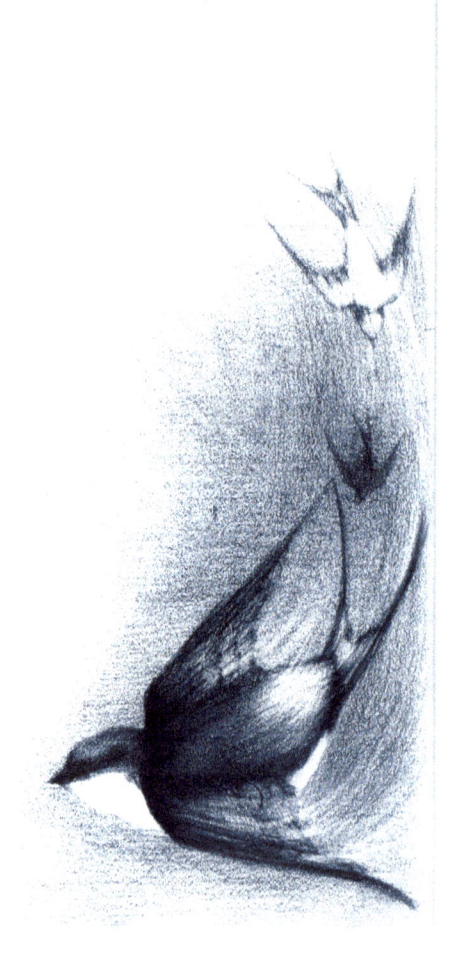

How to Read My Poems

I am an ordinary guy living a middle class life. I may imagine what it would be like to put on a wingsuit and jump off a mountain, but my stock-in-trade is the exploration of "everyday mind." I look for transcendent meaning in the ordinary happenings of daily life. I write in the morning everyday, and try to distill experience down to essentials. It is easy to overlook the instant-by-instant process of seeing, thinking, and responding to life — but in reality that is what life is.

The mind is self-interested and driven by powerful emotions. I look around and determine what to do. I judge what's worthy, and establish a list of priorities. My likes and dislikes become signposts, and if I am not careful I find myself repeating a pattern of behavior, and get stuck, narrowly seeing, feeling, experiencing — and then where is novelty?

Spring has sprung but today is chilly. I love watching the seasons change in a succession of little details, because the seasons are so much bigger than what's going on in my mind. There is always a lot going on in nature, and my practice is to open, so that more of reality may penetrate my consciousness.

I practice opening my awareness to the world inside and outside of me. Consciousness is a miracle — but I have to learn how to use the gift of Consciousness. This is what my poetry is about.

My daughter, Jocelyn MacDonald, is a wonderful artist. Her art work graces this book.

I am Barry MacDonald. I received the *dharma* name, *Tekkan*, which means, Iron Man, a settled practitioner of great determination.

— *Tekkan*

Everyday Mind XII

The sun this morning
is fierce enough
to burn its shining disk
right through a layer
of clouds.

I am wearing a straw hat with a wide
Brim shielding my eyes from the rising sun —
And if I had a boss he would not be
Happy with me because I look to be

Almost completely idle — my fingers
Are poised over the keyboard but I'm not
Typing — or I am flicking my fingers
Out in sequence from a fist as I am

Counting syllables — sitting at my desk
Facing a window — attempting to catch
Something extraordinary in the air
Or a usable fact from Google but

The sun is rising in an open sky
And what's so interesting about that?

The sun's not rising —
the earth is rolling in
the direction of
the sun at about a
thousand miles an hour.

This morning was darker than normal and
I noticed the clouds were heavy and low
As I went about brushing and feeding
My cats and cleaning the cat litter box

And my mind became fully awake as
The warm water cascaded over my
Naked body in the shower — and I
Explored possibilities for the day —

I heard the rain begin to fall through the
Open windows of my room — as I was
Sitting cross-legged on a cushion in
The dark — the rain accumulated in

A pattering of drops falling on the
Roof and grass — rising to a crescendo.

Yesterday afternoon
a moist heat
clung to my skin but
this morning there is
enveloping coolness.

When the sun is up on a summer day
And the shadows of the trees and buildings —
And the shadows of the people walking
Are making such a sharp contrast — and when

The leaves are rustling in a wind and
The river is undulating and the
Steel frame of the Lift Bridge in downtown
Stillwater is brilliantly reflecting

The sun with razor clarity — then the
Shadows offer no relief from the heat
Of daylight and then who notices the
Silhouettes of the shadows shrinking to

A minimum under the midday height
Of the summer sun burning so brightly?

The blazing sun
would be beyond
experience
unknowable
without
shadows.

I was helping Jocelyn and Eric
Move to Minneapolis by backing
My car up a hill of a driveway to
Their apartment — when I came to a

Point of turning to avoid another
Car — and I had to guess direction
Because I can't see over the rear of
My car — and crunch — I hit the other car —

I jumped out to inspect the damage which
Was nothing to the other bumper and
I really did think there was no damage
To my bumper either — and as no one

Was watching I rubbed out the scuffmarks and
Decided to pretend nothing happened.

Jocelyn saw a
dent and Eric laid
on the ground and popped
the fiberglass corner out
and I professed ignorance.

The car that I tried to avoid belonged
To my ex-wife Yoshiko who was there
To help move our daughter Jocelyn — and
I know how much Yoshiko cherishes

Her car — and there was the time in Japan
When I ate a glob of wasabi — which
Is a very hot sauce meant to be used
With sparing discretion — that I thought was

Guacamole — with the result that I
Nearly blew my head off — and the mishap
Is never forgotten — and the story
Is often retold — so I could assume

That my accident while backing up would
Live on in infamy forevermore.

While backing up and
having to guess at
distances I knew
the difficulty
but I was cocky.

[Yoshiko is pronounced Yosheeko]

Just by virtue of taking a risk I
Propelled myself on an unexpected
Rollercoaster ride of daring and of
Panic and of the fear of exposure

And of sudden relief when I believed
I escaped and nothing had happened — and
When I wet the tips of my fingers with
Spit and rubbed out the scuff marks truly my

Calm was reestablished — but Jocelyn
Saw right away what had eluded me —
That there was a fresh dent in the bumper
Of my Toyota Corolla — I was

Even a little jealous that Eric
Knew how to pop away the evidence.

Nothing more was said
and now I will see
if Jocelyn is really
reading the poems
I've been emailing.

It was about 3 in the morning I
Think when I got up from bed to go to
The bathroom to pee — which is my habit —
And then I returned to the bedroom and

Closed the door — and then either I can fall
Asleep again — or if unlucky — I
Can't and I toss about for the rest
Of the night — but this night I noticed a

Rustle at the open window and realized
Kitcat was in the room — but I was too
Tired to rise again and grab him so I
Just tried to sleep — and I almost managed to

Doze off but I was held in suspension
Because I knew Kitcat was in the room.

Kitcat is a
rascal and a fool
and he is most attentive
to outside noises
and most jumpy at night.

I think there was a sunlit beach with a
Plethora of bodacious women in
The skimpiest of bikinis in the
Dream that I left behind me when I rose

To pee — and now I was on the edge of
Rejoining them with hardly a whisper of
A breeze in the room when at the open
Window just above my head I heard a

Shifting of the curtains and I knew that
Kitcat was alert and surveying the
Night for danger — in the middle of a
Careless jumble I almost managed to

Conk but part of me was aware that a
Tense and nervy Kitcat was in the room.

Was I dreaming
of restless leopards
on the savanna
of Africa or was I
elsewhere?

There is a window on the south side of
The room and a window on the east just
Above the head of my bed and in my
Dazed and dozing state I knew that Kit was

Slinking between the windows as the air
Was cool and tranquilizing — which always
Makes me think of those midsummer night dreams
That Shakespeare goes on about — and I was

Drifting and swinging as if I were in
A hammock and then I felt that Kitcat
Was standing on my legs and he broke the
Spell of slumbering and I awoke and

Knew that the opportunity was gone
And the only thing to do was to write.

I recognize when
the facility for
putting words together
arrives — and I won't
squander opportunity.

There is a window on the south side of
The room and a window on the east just
Above the head of my bed and in my
Dazed and dozing state I knew that Kit was

Slinking between the windows as the air
Was cool and tranquilizing — which always
Makes me think of those midsummer night dreams
That Shakespeare goes on about — and I was

Drifting and swinging as if I were in
A hammock and then I felt that Kitcat
Was standing on my legs and he broke the
Spell of slumbering and I awoke and

Knew that the opportunity was gone
And the only thing to do was to write.

I recognize when
the facility for
putting words together
arrives — and I won't
squander opportunity.

I first heard about meditation by
Reading Hermann Hesse's Siddhartha
In my high school library — and I was
Captivated by the mysterious

Spiritual journey Siddhartha embarked
Upon — that he left a luxurious
Life in a quest for enlightenment in
The jungle of India two thousand

Years ago — that he bore the hardships of
Living naked in the rain the heat and
The cold and that he endured the rigors
Of hunger — that he would willingly do

This by straightening his back and crossing
His legs — and by going into a trance.

I wanted the
superhuman
experience of
enlightenment
and the trance.

Hermann Hesse planted a seed that flowered
When I arrived in Japan twenty years
Later to be an English teacher and
A friend introduced me to a temple

And I was initiated into
The way of Zen — and I learned how to sit
Quietly with a straight back and crossed legs
While the monks and the visitors sat for

Many hours of a day for seven days
Of meditation — and the Zen master
Said that I had entered Buddha way
And that the point of the practicing is

To awaken and I could not fail if
I were wholehearted in my efforts.

During seven days
of enveloping quiet
there were bells
and drums and people
stepped carefully.

I discovered that my idea of
Meditation as a trance I enter
Or a spell I cast upon myself was
Mistaken — and that the purpose of the

Posture and the surrounding quiet was
For me to experience clearly the
Ordinary operation of my
Mind — so that I could see the restlessness

And could understand the fabrications
That I invent to explain the world to
Me — so that I could appreciate that
So much of my thinking is leading me

Astray — and that I am the author of
My dissatisfaction and confusion.

The world becomes
a funhouse mirror
of the way I am
thinking and
feeling.

My mind is a bowl responding in the
Dark absorbing vibrations and raising
A radiant sun — and creating the
Jubilant celebration of the birds —

Straightening my spine and crossing my legs
I don't have to do anything extra
Because my retina and synapses
Are inventing the sunlight — my eardrums

And synapses are devising bird song —
Because without the bowl of my mind the
Vibrations in the air would obtain no
Response — and without the vibrations in

The air my magical bowl would become
Empty — and what would emptiness be like?

My mind is a bowl
inventing the cosmos —
the cosmos is
vibration
creating
me.

I was sitting at a booth selling books
And watching people going by and most
Were indifferent but some would stop and
Talk for a while when a girl walked by who

I was happy to give two years of predawn
Attention to — when we talked for an hour
On the phone every day — while I was in
Bed — and we shared our emotions and talked

About the people we knew and I learned
How intoxicating conversation
Could be — enough to occupy me for
The rest of my days — but she kept walking

And I didn't try to stop her and I
Am not even sure whether she saw me.

She reminded me
I can choose to
reinterpret
events endlessly
but I'd rather not.

When I put my thermos of coffee down
And can't remember where I put it or
When I suddenly meet someone I know
And I find I can't remember his name

My thoughts are condemning of myself for
My poor memory — but then there are the
Regretful experiences when I
Invested so much hopeful emotion

With perhaps some unwise expectation
And a good measure of blind fantasy
In a pursuit that I knew was risky — then
I find that forgetting isn't easy

And the weight of unresolved memory
Is a ferment of continuing pangs.

Dropping rain
bubbling springs
fleeting rivers
falling water
boundless oceans
clouds drifting
have no memory.

These are the riddles of consciousness to
Wonder — was there a beginning — is there
An end — did I originate at birth —
Do I have a destination — because

Everything is moving — the galaxies
The stars and the planets are orbiting —
Starlight penetrates the cosmos in waves —
Subatomic particles are spinning —

The sun enfolds my face in a warm glow
And sometimes I feel perfectly at home —
But sometimes I am overcome with a
Sense of urgency that I have to make

Something happen — but then I realize —
I'm not at all sure what I really want.

Today I'm
drinking coffee
reading essays
absorbing news
answering mail.

How weary would I be trailing behind
Me the unerring memories of lives
With the intervals of prosperity
And the endurance of the heartbreaking

Turns of fortune — when there were too many
Disappointments — when in my misery
I could not stop comparing myself with
Others who were luckier — and what would

Remembering a lover who is lost
To me forever be like — as I could
Not forget her gentleness and voice —
Wouldn't I be better off forgetting

Every detail of my experience
Whether I was jubilant or burdened?

Maybe misplacing
my car keys
is a touch
of grace?

Where is he? I asked as I hadn't seen
Him for several weeks and I missed his smile
And his warm intelligence — and she took
Me aside where the others couldn't hear

And answered that he's been on a bender
And she doesn't know what to do and would
I call him she asked as she knows he and
I are friends — I remember he isn't

The first alcoholic she's been involved
With and I recognize desperation
When I see it — set apart where others
Can't see it — because with the others she

Is smiling and putting on a brave face
As I see both of them are suffering.

"Yes I'll call and
remember you
didn't cause it
can't control it
can't cure it."

There is freedom in the moment to think
About whatever comes to mind and not
To dwell upon what's beyond my sight and what's
Surpassing my ability to change

As I could be preoccupied with an
Alcoholic friend who can't stop drinking
Or I could be wondering how my son
Is faring in Alaska but after

Reaching out and not hearing news there is
Nothing more to do — and every moment
I could be encumbered uselessly or
I could deploy my daily routines and

Drink my coffee and edit some essays
And lose myself in intriguing details.

A gray sparrow
is hopping in the
hedge outside the
window a couple
feet away.

When I doubt myself the people and the
Events of a day become funhouse mirrors
Reflecting back to me my supposed
Image distorted by what I think should

Be happening — and a debate ensues
Wherein part of me justifies myself
While the other part wants a convincing
Satisfaction that's unobtainable —

But I've experienced enough to know
The internal dialogue is useless
And a friendly honest conversation
About any topic that comes to mind

Dissolves the mirrors and clarifies my
Vision — and life returns to normalcy.

A distorted
perspective dissolves
with friendly
conversation with
another person.

Down corridors and into the rooms of
What are more often than not churches — and
This was true even for the nine years that
I lived in Japan — I will go to meet my

Fellow alcoholics who are trying
To stay sober — and for more than thirty
Years we have shared the camaraderie
Of getting to know each others' stories

And of learning the tricks of avoiding
The first drink — which is the drink leading to
Catastrophe — and you wouldn't know it
Being with us as a nonalcoholic

And witnessing our banter and laughter
That some of us are fighting to survive.

At some point we are
desperadoes and despite
our laughter we need
to remember the
initial desperation.

As we were walking Jane took off her shoes
And went barefoot on the sidewalk — which I
Could never have predicated and I said
So — and then she deliberately sped up

With her long legs flowing forcing me to
Keep up — and I inquired wasn't she
Worried about stepping on debris on
The concrete — and she scoffed saying there was

No debris because someone always comes
By to sweep it away especially
Near the state capitol building to which
I replied there is debris too small to

Be seen everywhere except on mountain
Tops and even there the rock will crumble.

She said something
unremarkable
but she did
get the last
word.

I want the child in me to emerge as
Often as possible as I let go
Of the tensions and the expectations
Coming with experience as I give

Myself the quiet allowing my thoughts
To settle down — seeing so to speak the
Operation of my thinking — that all
The emotions come and go if they are

Given the room to express themselves and
Seeing so to speak I don't have to cling
To a point of view — and when I let go
I can dwell again in child-like wonder

As life becomes a ceaseless adventure
Full of unpredictable potential.

So much tension is
expectation run
amok dreading
unavoidable
conclusions.

The serried fields of corn are fully grown
The days are almost equally balanced
Between showers of the rain and sunshine
And in the afternoon there is the moist

Embrace of summer humidity and
The air is filled in the evening with
The pestering of flying insects but
Here and there about the country in the

Upper reaches of the trees there are the
First appearances of the red leaves of
Autumn and there is no denying now
That darkness is encroaching day after

Day further into the daylight and yet
Winter seems an impossibility.

Something about the
constancy of the clouds
sailing across the sky
merges the seasons
together in memory.

I dreamed of being a mite on a walk
Across the palm of a sleeping human's
Hand encountering successive creases
And deep lines in the dark — and I could choose

To follow along the pathway of one
Of the smaller creases while indulging
A belief that a destination were
Ahead — but then eventually I

Would come across the deepest of lines and
Be forced to descend the depth with an
Ominous premonition that I was
Being channeled having only the choice

Of moving forward to uncertainty
Or of stopping and awaiting my fate.

But perspective
easily shifts with
the brilliance of
the morning light.

Sometimes when entering a room I will
Discover that I've forgotten why I
Came — and at other times I will see a
Familiar person and realize

That I can't remember his name — and then
I think myself unworthy and wonder
Whether I should stand within the tall grass
To attract the ticks — but sometimes I will

See or hear something triggering a
Memory and precipitously I
Am reliving the circumstances
And rehashing the arguments of a

Cherished grudge of a dozen years ago
And I think forgetting would be blissful.

Forgetting and
remembering
are things I do
without thinking
much about them.

The sun of this morning brightens all of
My sensations and fosters clarity
And all the ups and downs involved in a
Typical season dissolve at sunrise

As the sun is a worthy symbol of
My sphere of consciousness bringing to light
Everything it touches enlivening
And enthusing with the combustion of

My attention — and problems left over
From yesterday are child's play to resolve
When energy and clarity are merged —
But I also need to recognize when

My energy is ebbing because then
The shadows assume their rightful places.

Shadow surrounds
incandescence —
forgetfulness
accompanies
clarity.

There's a short sleeve shirt that's a pleasure to
Wear once the mornings become chilly in
August because it's a thick weave and has
The substance to keep the warmth inside and

It is a black silk shirt embroidered with
Navy blue tracery and luminous
Silver dragons that for some reason leads
Me to think of stardust and gravity

As if it were a representation
Of the primordial cosmos swirling
And coalescing into galaxies
Containing the code of consciousness and

When wearing it I feel like royalty
Representing the life of the cosmos.

It was an eight-dollar
purchase at the
second-hand store
called Good Will in
Stillwater Minnesota.

I want to rethink my attitude towards
Forgetfulness — while stipulating that
Forgetting a name or misplacing my
Car keys will always be irritating —

Because on occasion when I awake
In the night remembering my regrets
Experiencing again frustrations
Searching again for consolation in

The darkness where imagination runs
Wild even as the recreation of
Vanished opportunity is tempting
I know my memory is distorted

And what could have happened differently
Isn't worth the useless speculation.

Forgetting is
opening
sleeping
dreaming
spontaneously.

I remember Zen master Harada
Saying if you know something — forget it —
Which sounds simple but is complicated
Because I don't like the embarrassment

Of forgetting someone's name — but then I
Wonder whether Harada was meaning
To forget the embarrassment that comes
With forgetting names — that I shouldn't be

Clinging to the idea that I am a
Person who habitually forgets
Names — that I should relax and not worry
No matter how many names I forget

Because if a person is important
Certainly I will remember the name.

I guess remembering
and forgetting go along
with the dissolving
and rebirthing of
everything.

Temple Hosshin-ji

Monks in the Zen temple were serious
During continuous meditation
And a strict schedule was enforced with the
Striking of the bells and wooden clappers

And there was no unnecessary talk
As we sat and ate and walked about in
Silence — as we were pursuing the trick
Of liberation desiring to cast

Away our bodies and minds to become
Enlightened penetrating instantly
The boundary between ignorance and
Certitude — study the moment — practice

Wholeheartedly — master Harada said —
Obtain the posture — and forget yourself.

Master Harada struck
the tatami with a staff —
saying with wholehearted
effort you cannot miss.

I frequently visited *Hosshin-ji*
Doing continuous meditation
Because I had a yen for Zen wanting
Liberation thinking I could grasp it

Through determination and focus — and
After six days of sitting I achieved
Such an energetic clarity that
Only comes from strenuous effort with

The knowledge that I could never do more
Through force of will — but my endurance of
The lotus posture wasn't enough to
Evade my ego — which I felt as a

Burden — so with alert exuberance
I left a little disoriented.

The exhortation of
Harada Sekkei Roshi
resembled the hectoring
of my wrestling coach —
had I failed?

I was an English teacher in Japan
And wasn't a monk but could arrange to
Visit four times a year — and I didn't
Wear the formal black robes but instead I

Gallivanted in my black pants and a
Black sweatshirt with a blue scarf unaware
Of the delicate sensibility
Of the monks passing silently about

With stern faces until the tallest monk
Daigaku Rumme came and leaned over
Me tucking the blazing blue of the scarf
Inside my sweat shirt and thus harmony

Was restored in the temple as I learned
That blue is distracting in the Zendo.

It's surprising
how often words
are unnecessary.

There is a curious rumbling of
Thunder in the distance while the sky was
Resplendent an hour ago — and now the
Prospect of an open morning is gone

And the gray of the clouds is an almost
Certain indication of rain coming —
Which would not have been a surprise if I
Were watching the satellite images

But sometimes I like the weather to come
Upon me unannounced by news people
Because surprising weather consists of
Raw experience — as a mixture of

Beauty alternating with the burdens
And unpredictability of life.

I don't dislike the rain
as the sound of rain is
pleasing — and soothing
spattering and drumming — and
I don't have to shovel rain.

When rummaging in the garage I found
Two sets of wind chimes I had put aside
Because they both were missing the part that
Catches the slightest of winds moving the

Center disk striking the chimes and making
The air resonate — and I shook the chimes
And heard the familiar falsetto
And the bass again after their many

Years of silence — their hooks under the eaves
Were there and I hung the chimes along my
Roof again resolving as I did to
Refashion the wind catchers when I could —

Windy days and chimes remind me of how
Simple and pleasurable beauty is.

A home
and
chimes
are
musical.

Master Harada reminded me of
My high school wrestling coach inspiring
Extraordinary efforts through the force
Of his personality — and he spoke

With admiration of a Zen master
Of a century ago who marshaled
The monks and pronounced that whomever had
Not grasped enlightenment by the end of

The practice period would be buried
Alive — and master Harada didn't
Reveal how many were actually
Covered up so I presume after the

Appointed time the temple was filled with
Realized followers of the Buddha.

Earnest effort
and humor
inspire
good practice.

Harada was reputed to be a
Teacher of koans — embedding nagging
Riddles within a mind — by remarking
With wholehearted effort attainment is

Like hitting the ground with a staff and you
Cannot miss — and those who fail deserve to
Be buried alive — and with the correct
Posture of mind in an instant you may

Forget yourself — and he energized and
Directed me and I struggled silently
By maintaining a straight back and crossed legs
Hour after hour day after day month

After month — laboring and desiring
To extinguish desire by force of will.

My wrestling coach
never imposed
enticing and
impossible
situations.

Mowing the grass weekly was what I did
Because I had to and viewed it as a
Chore but now I'm liking the exercise
And am circling the flower gardens

I established by placing large rocks in
Ovals about the yard — mowing around
The rocks once and twice and thrice pretending
I am a star spiraling about the

Milky Way rotating further out with
Each pass participating in the swirl
Of gravity grateful to have a small
Portion of the earth to care about and

Not presumptuous that the living earth is
Something that is permanently possessed.

I pass over the
entirety — about the
gardens apple trees
cottonwood pines and the house —
with a pair of whirling blades.

Saying hippopotamus is lovely
And saying hippopotami is a
Wonderful variation with the
Added benefit that people may not

Understand the meaning — and I enjoy
Pronouncing hippopotamus with an
Ascending inflection as if I were
Asking a question — and it's fun to say

Hippopotamus while putting on a
Stern expression because it makes such a
Curious contrast with the gaiety of
The word — and you should try saying every

Syllable pausing in-between because
You'll find it difficult not to speed up.

It's regrettable
there aren't many
occasions in
America to say
hip-po-potamus.

In the last few day of summer I took
A walk to the horizon and on the way
There were the grasshoppers and crickets and
When I reached the mile long avenue in

The sky of the Crossing Bridge with the broad
River a hundred feet below me I
Wondered how the construction workers spanned
The empty air with steel and concrete when

There was as yet nowhere to stand — and on
Returning I thought of the sayings of
The Zen masters — that I do not exist —
That my hand is illusory grasping

At smoke — that I can't discover the way
Either by doing or by not doing.

A thousand years ago
the Chinese monks walked great
distances searching for a
master of Zen who could
spark them.

I am a sphere of consciousness shining
The light of my awareness over the
Events of every day — and even when
Remembering I am remembering

Presently so what I remember is
An illusion — and when indulging my
Memories I am recreating what
Happened and using memories often

To make myself happy or remorseful —
And in continuing if not careful
I will be beholding a series of
Funhouse mirrors each as distorted as

Another as the emotion of the
Present moment is most dominating.

The sky and
the diversity of
clouds are more
worthy of
attention.

The monkey bars in the empty park were
Inviting — could I grip and hold and
Swing my body's weight with alternating
Hands propelling myself to the end — yes

I could and did — in junior high school our
Gym teacher led the boys onto the bus
While we were wearing our white t-shirts
Shorts and — for the first time ever — jockstraps —

While going to the Old Athletic Field
And preparing for competition
Gangly and short and chubby and nervous
And unprepared for public exposure —

The adrenalin of excitement and
Embarrassment was intoxicating.

I can do the monkey bars
today but my fellows
outdo me by taking
expensive vacations in
Paris or the Bahamas.

There are ten thousand leaves moving in a
Gentle breeze in the September light of
A morning sunrise as the peaking of
The summer heat is passing by and the

Season is approaching a natural
Harvesting of the growth of the rooted
Plants — and the light shining on the green leaves
Is a sight worthy of noticing and

Cherishing — as the leaves are bearing the
Bite marks of the insects and soon the leaves
Will be turning into autumn colors
And yet the quality of September

Light is most beautiful I think as the
Light isn't starkly bright but is glowing.

Shadow is lengthening
further into daylight
and shadow is gathering
underneath the trees when the
sky is overcome with clouds.

When the cosmos was spontaneously
Birthing there was no bang because there were
No ears to hear the sound and no air to
Transmit the vibrations — and even now

Outside of the earth's atmosphere within
The vacuum of space the original
Silence is predominating — but I
Am a drop of consciousness and the

Earth also is a drop of consciousness —
And when I am sitting quietly and
Attending to my thoughts and listening
To the sounds of the birds or of the rain I

Am not separate from the primal
Impetus but continuous with it.

From the silence
reverberations of
pattering rain and
singing birds have
emerged.

The nastiness of the political
Discourse broadcast on the cable channels
On the radio and in newspapers
Is frightening — and because I attend

To the details of events and issues
I can identify the smears the lies
The distortions and the propaganda
I can see how the youngest voters are

Programmed to hate before they understand
The history and the complexity
Of government — as politicos are
Masterful at deceiving innocence

At manipulating ignorance and
At camouflaging insincerity.

Once a person is
poisoned with aggressive
talking points reasoned
dialogue becomes
almost impossible.

I practice Zen to separate my
Emotions from the vitriol of
The cultural and political war
That is raging across America

As I am writing and publishing on
Current events — and having already
Informed myself about the destructive
And dominating aspects of money

Power and government nothing about
Today's poisonous discourse surprises
Me — except perhaps the extent to which
Politicos are eager to involve

Children from the grade schools through the high schools —
Teaching partisan ideology.

No segment of
society is free of
the taint of politics —
not even the *dharma*
in Zen centers.

No matter how justified it appears
With every ounce of vigor to oppose
The haters in society using
Accusatory language is risky

Because hating will mirror hating in
Opposition with the escalating
Rhetoric transforming into vengeance —
And there are battles to be fought and won —

But once belligerence has taken root
Distinguishing honest disagreement
From malicious intent is difficult
And vengeful words are poisonous to those

Who say them because we don't realize
Hating haters turns us into haters.

Governing involves
the use of power and
the allocation of
precious commodities
conjuring disagreement.

It is a goofy frog painted yellow
And green that is hanging on the outside
Of the door that's an entrance into my
House — it was put there by my ex-wife whom

I allowed to live with me for six years
Following our divorce — though there really
Wasn't a reconciliation but
Only a toleration that has worn

Out — that has resulted in me asking
Her to leave the home — which grieves me to do —
Which she is unable to understand —
I hope her leaving eventually

Will be seen to be the best outcome for
Both of us — even if it's painful now.

Yoshiko bought
the frog with
the script saying
welcome.

A generation has passed — the children
Are grown and gone — my home is cluttered with
Useless things — and I want to rent a large
Dumping container and like a cyclone

Progress through the bookshelves closets cupboards
Wardrobes chests of drawers — look under the beds
Into boxes untouched for years — enter the
Spare room and drag the mattress up the stairs

Out through the door — I will break the couch
We had such trouble getting into the
Basement into pieces and throw it out
Bit by bit — but perhaps I'm not prepared

To be so determinate when finding
The wedding and the honeymoon photos.

In a corner of
the ceiling there are
bits of crepe paper
streamers left from
a birthday party.

Thousands of memories of Yoshiko
Are embedded and latent in my mind
Ready to emerge and surprise me — as
Someone in a conversation mentioned

The Renaissance Fair and I remembered
The day we went as a family when
She decided my presence in the group
Wasn't wanted and she excluded me —

And I realize the emotion of
What I thought was guilt — in asking her to
Leave — is probably grieving — as I had
Already lost my family many

Years ago — as our togetherness was
A façade concealing my loneliness.

Guilt and grieving
are mixed and
justification
isn't necessary.

By the river in downtown Stillwater
There is a planter full of purple and
Red petunias blooming in the sunlight
Escaping my notice until today

I plucked a blossom — felt the velvety
Texture — inhaled the petunia scent —
Red and purple richness — soft petals — the
Balm of inhaling petunias — surprised

Me — and yes I noticed sunlight playing
On the surface of the river and the
Dewdrops sprinkled on the newly mown grass
But they were insignificant today

I asked a passerby for the flower's
Name — and now I know about petunias.

My tongue
dances when
I say
petunia.

After thirty years of living every
Drawer and closet is full of stuff some of
Which I haven't handled for twenty years —
Like the fifty-year-old sleeping bags I

Inherited from my parents — I am
Preparing to be a cyclone tossing
Everything time has rendered useless but
I am dreading triggering the landmines

Like deciding what to do with the
Sturdy bags we used on our honeymoon
How to dispose of the wedding photos —
It would be better not to look at them —

I will be sorting the debris of life
Touching items — enduring memory.

I am preparing to
rediscover
relive
reflect
renew.

When I am unable to sleep sometimes
At night I will hear the horn of a train
In the distance — and when I am sitting
Before dawn absorbing the sounds through my

Window I will hear traffic moving on
The highway and on the city streets — then
I remember meditating before
Dawn in a temple in a city on

A bay by the Sea of Japan where I
Heard the traffic in the distance on
The highway — people are always moving
Restlessly in the dark in the distance

Adopting a direction — departing
And arriving at their destinations.

People are moving
in the night covering
distances going
somewhere in
solitude.

Waves of light are speeding while waves of sound
Are leisurely and our classic Rolls Royce
Is loitering on the highway passing
Tractor-trailer trucks over the rolling

Hills as we are seeing the fully grown
Rows of corn and grass moving in a breeze
And shining in the mild light of early
September — as we are progressing to

The Log Cabin Family Restaurant in
Baraboo Wisconsin again for our
Periodic business meeting where we
Discuss the shifting fortunes of our work —

A political movement has died and
We are conniving to launch another.

We are caught in a swirl
orbiting and waving
ceasing and beginning
conversing and silent
continuing.

No — the supervisor said — we need the
Security code that your ex-wife made
Twenty years ago before we will stop
The billing and will discontinue

Your Internet services — and thank you
For your patience — but you are sending the
Code to my ex-wife's email address and
I don't have access to that address now

I replied — and I'm waiting for it to
Arrive by mail but it's not coming and
I don't want penalties for late payments
And don't want my credit rating ruined

And why can't you be adaptable and
Send it to my current email address?

Rules are rules and
it's easy to
initiate services
and hard to break the bonds of
connectivity.

On the refrigerator there is a
Piece of paper left behind announcing
The award that my ex-wife Yoshiko was
Given for being the best employee of

The month — and I know she's a hard worker
And that everyone who was working at
The hotel where Yoshiko cleaned rooms has
Left the hotel — even the owners and

Managers — have gone on to better jobs
Years ago — and I don't know where she is
Don't know whether she is struggling or
Doing well — she wouldn't believe me if

I told her but I grieve for the hardness
Of her life — and want her to be happy.

I will enclose the
award in a box
containing photos
of the family growing
until today.

I don't remember what the arguments
Were about but only that they happened
And that they happened for thirty-three years
Within intervals approximating

Companionship and even happiness
On occasion when I was proud to be
A Dad and a provider — but trauma from
Her childhood never healed — her anger and

Her accusatory mentality
Are a burden I can no longer carry —
Who's right or wrong is trivial — the fact
Is we don't get along and we need to

Live separately for our closing years
And maybe we can both be happier.

Living together for
six years after
a twenty-seven marriage
ended in divorce
was a mistake.

There is space within my house created
By the dispersal of my family
And the only disagreement now is
Where the cat litter box belongs and that

Will involve negotiation between
My felines and me — I am adjusting
To the reliable quiet within
The rooms I know so well — I am aware

Of the potential for remorse and grief
To take over the decisions about
What to keep or to let go — the present
Is pregnant with possibility and

I think the sky is a good example —
Cloudy or empty — it is full of light.

Life-giving energy
permeates being
constantly
vibrating
here.

In September I notice the little
Kids on the corner waiting for the bus
To take them to school — remembering as
I do the many years I took the bus to

School — recalling the apprehension and
The unpredictability coming
With leaving home for the first time and of
Encountering the presence of strangers —

And today I notice the little kids
With a father or mother beside them
Undergoing as they are the first pains
Of separation realizing the

Bonds of parentage — that no matter how
Long I live I will always be a Dad.

Attending grade school
junior high and high school
for the second time with
my kids I watched them
grow and leave home.

A zebra was injured and unable
To rise from the grass of the savanna
When in the distance a lion appeared
And the lion began to approach at

A trot — the features of the lion's face
Expressed a stern intensity and the
Mane surrounding his face was flowing with
The motion of his advance — while the tall

Grass obscured the movement of his legs the
Shaggy mane and face were fascinating
Coming from a distance as his face was
Alert and fixed with brutal intention —

There is an awful and mesmerizing
Ruthlessness in an apex predator.

I remember being
fascinated by the
gleaming brass of a
lion's face fashioned
into a door knocker.

I am leaving my windows open just
A little above the sill overnight
Regardless of the chill encroaching in
The night — because I am holding on to

The ease of the warmer days and there is
A visceral revulsion to the coming
Season — in the morning I am walking
About in bare feet — though my ankles are

Cooler and the wood boards of the floor are
Are beginning to impart a bite through
The soles of my feet and up my legs — I'm
Not going to shut my windows and seal my

House until it's really necessary
When I have to resort to the furnace.

The afternoon sun
is warm and so many
green leaves are
reflecting a
golden light.

Love and the absence of love are woven
Together as I thought I knew what was
Missing and told myself for years if she
Weren't here I'd have what I want — but I am

Discovering all the time and beneath
My conscious awareness I was blaming
Her for an absence of love while knowing
She was wounded and suffering from her

Torturous thoughts as I was defensive
And withdrawn and was incapable of
Providing beyond the shelter of a
House which really didn't amount to a

Home — and now hunger is mixed with numbness
And I have no idea what I want.

There is love
to be seen in people's
faces in their movements
and in the generations
of children.

We arise from the waves and orbits of
Particles spinning and winking in and
Out of existence — from the emptiness
From which everything emerges — and we

Arise on a rotating and orbiting
Planet in a solar system within
A galaxy along with the other
Galaxies as all the galaxies are

Expanding — moving and thinking within
The cycles of seconds and minutes and
Hours days seasons and years — and it's easy
Not to notice the segmentation of

Time and distance are artificial tools
Measuring underlying emptiness.

The movement
of second and hour hands
around a clock are
only meaningful
to human minds.

The outermost layer is thin and dry
And is not edible so I make a
Cut and peel the layer off — I cut the
Whole in halves with a heavy blade — and with

My fingers holding the ends together
I cut across a half to make slices —
Then comes the tricky part as I'm holding
The slices of the half together with

My fingers as I'm cutting lengthwise
And aiming to produce smaller sections
And to put them in the crock pot when it
Just happens that my fingers fumble and

Everything falls apart forcing me to
Say — I can't cut an onion gracefully.

The second half is
especially
troublesome
as my eyes are
burning with tears.

There are three curio cabinets in
My home holding porcelain figurines
Of Chinese monks and stone frogs untouched for
Twenty years because the keys were broken

Or lost — the dust has settled within them
Coating the glass and ornaments — people
Applied effort and skill to create the
Cabinets and artwork but today I

Avoid looking at them — the debris in
My life has accumulated and needs
Careful attention — time and energy —
Patience and sorting through to discover

What's worth keeping — what should be discarded —
As most of what I have just collects dust.

Every decision
over everything
will be a rearrangement
and a paring down of
superfluity.

A home contains the habits of those who
Live within it and my cats every night
Would sleep in her room with her as I was
Left in blissful solitude — and as her

Absence is being felt with the days and
Weeks I've been watching the cats to see how
They would respond — when Henry who seldom
Attended to me looked in my eyes with

Inquiry as if to say — where is she —
When Kitcat wandered throughout the house while
Yowling as he was not in the habit
Of doing beforehand — though with Johnnie

I'm not observing any difference
But I'm not sure that means he doesn't care.

Henry and Johnnie
like to take the space in the
center of the bed
so I have to push them off —
Kitcat wanders in the night.

There is a chilly dampness about the
Air and the gray sky is imposing a
Somberness over the morning as I
Am driving and noticing the orange

And red scattered among the green leaves in
Stillwater — as I am absorbing yet
Another turning of the seasons with
A recycling of sights I've seen so

Many times before — accumulating
A weightiness and grandeur with the years
Knowing the orbits within the orbits
The earth and the sun are subject to — I

Feel the repetition and the impact
Of time incessantly recreating.

And yet there is a
poignancy about
these days about my
dissolving family which
is a new experience.

It's early in autumn but the robins
Have already left and are migrating
To sunnier landscapes a friend told me —
Also saying that robins migrate in

Flocks — which was news to me — it's easy not
To notice the absence of the robins
As they are a tiny detail of the
Air and the sky among the millions of

Cyclical changes in a season — I
Notice the robins singing at sunrise
And pecking at the earthworms in puddles
Collecting in my driveway after a

Soaking shower during the spring — but there
Are so many things to see in summer.

The robins aren't separate
from the air and sky
but are always a part of
the air and sky — even if
they're not here.

I'm hosting my subscribers and donors
To a dinner and speech at a fancy
Restaurant hoping to generate the
Donations necessary for success

Our speaker is an expert on healthcare
And two judges a senator and a
Mayor are attending — we oppose the
Tentacles of the bureaucratic state

Resisting the crushing octopus of
Mandates and regulations resulting
In waiting lists and rationing — we are
Intelligent and enthusiastic

And we share a belief in liberty
Which is weakening in America.

The magazine I
publish is laboring
against the tide of
dominating
opinion.

I could write continuous lines about
Economic and bureaucratic facts
Arguing what I believe is the most
Humane point of view — but regardless of

My intentions I'd only engender
Disagreement — and my offerings would
Not amount to poetry — arguments and
Bitterness and confusion are part of

Society — with coalitions of
People trying to get the better of
Other people — and yet companionship
And love and art and music are also

Part of society as we oscillate
Between belligerence and harmony.

I am part
rascal
part lover
depending on
viewpoints.

A prominent politician's son is
Placed on the board of directors of a
Foreign energy company while the
Politician is in position to

Influence the course of business — even
Though the son has no expertise
Or experience to qualify for
The job — the business prospers and the son

Reaps millions of dollars in a few years
While a trickle of information is
Reported — but the vitriol of a
Swarm of journalists is diverted from

The politician and the son onto
Those who are exposing the corruption.

The politician claims
to be a champion
for the little guy
and a crusader
against corruption.

Judging by the indifference of the
Nation's top media watchdogs to the
Evidence of the obvious pay for
Play dealings of government officials

Corruption and hypocrisy are part
Of the game — as long as the practice is
Artfully concealed — but America
Is thought to be different — we believe

In liberty and justice — both parties
Profess to champion the little guy —
To force the billionaires to pay fairly
For the upkeep of the unfortunate —

But even within the United States
The ruling class is protecting itself.

Playing with words
generates joy and
enthusiasm while
watching politics
makes me tired.

The Big Dipper appears in the Northern
Sky — near the horizon in fall and high
In summer — the pattern was discovered
To be a bear by tribal ancestors

In Canada who said every autumn
Warriors hunt the bear and the green leaves
Are spattered by the bloody wounds of the
Bear — the ancient Phoenicians mariners

Navigated by the Dipper stars — and
Astronomers say in twenty-five thousand
Years the Big Dipper will be similar —
Even though the stars are incessantly

Moving and each star is variously
Distant — and dozens of light years away.

The stars are expanding
the mountains and hills are
rising and falling
like the waves of a
cosmic ocean.

They keep their appointed rounds about the
City streets — beginning before the dawn —
Witnessing the rising sun — enduring
Blizzards in winter — rain in spring — sticky

Air in summer — directing such massive
Vehicles and marshaling hundreds of
Horsepower engines — projecting power —
Revving their engines up and down — starting

And stopping — I see them on the hilly
Streets of Stillwater — standing while they are
Driving their trucks — as if piloting a
Ocean-going vessel over rolling

Swells — I imagine they are flexible
By bending their knees — rising and falling.

Garbage truck drivers
are unappreciated heroes
directing such
mechanized marvels.

If the space inside of an atom is
Ninety-nine percent empty — and if
The distance from the nucleus of the
Atom to the outer orbits of the

Atom's whirling electrons defining
The atom's size is comparable to
The pitcher's mound and the outer expanse
Of a baseball stadium — then all the

Things appearing in the world are mostly
Empty and we might be able to say
The world is mostly an illusion — but
While driving across an intersection

I was — smacked — by another vehicle
And my car spun around in a circle.

The impact left
me dazed and with
difficulty I focused on
the other driver's
insurance card.

I was looking for a parking place in
Minneapolis while all the streets were
Congested — driving parallel and one
Block over from a busy avenue

And I don't recall before the impact
Whether I stopped and looked before crossing
The intersection — but because it is
My habit to do so I assume I

Stopped and looked — and he clobbered my rear tire
On the passenger side spinning my car
Two hundred eighty degrees around — the
Impact was an absorbing sensation

Unlike anything I've experienced
Overloading and befuddling me.

Liability is a
word insurance companies
toss about — but I believe
he was
speeding.

Onions are ambrosia to the tongue
Melting to almost nothing inside of
My crock-pot while suffusing the corn
The cauliflower broccoli beef and

Mushrooms with flavor — an onion is a
Symbol of life — layer over layer
And day after day or year after year
And at the center nothing left over

And though I am harried with things to do
And I am giving my energy to
The pivotal decisions — and I am
Neglecting my sensibilities — I

Hope the day will finally come when
I learn to be an adequate cook.

I learned the
French method for
cutting onions — don't
cut the halves the way through
to keep from fumbling.

Rain was falling sporadically through the
Afternoon but I needed to cut and
Bag the hostas and daylilies — so I
Wore a warm jacket hat and gloves and used

A hedge trimmer making easy work of
The yearly ritual marking a turn
Into winter — moving from plant to plant
Cutting raking bagging taking bags to

The street — attending only to simple
Activity taking somber pleasure
In the task pulling and bending with my
Arms and legs — my mind didn't wander much —

Overhead — mother-of-pearl sky — about
Me — trees were wearing their party colors.

In the soreness and
difficulty moving
my back and legs on
the morning afterwards
there is satisfaction.

Night is encroaching into daylight and
Shadow is obscuring the apple trees —
The brilliant light and gentle breezes are
Migrating with the formations of geese

Flying south — the windows are shut and the
Furnace is humming and I am wearing
Socks for warmth while walking on the floorboards
Of my home — but there is a radiance

Penetrating the overcast sky as
I can see that the gray clouds are glowing
As the memory of all the winter
Skies I've ever seen are so familiar

But a radiance is persisting and
Penetrating another cloudy day.

No matter how cold
and overcast the
day the sky will be
radiant with the
ever-present light.

Waves of light are very fast — waves of sound
Are slower — the pull and release of tides
Are reliable — the cycles of the
Moon and the rotation of the earth are

Constant — seasons are repetitive and
Yet the dispersion of the leaves and the
Withdrawal of warmth comes with shock that life
Is getting serious now — it's time to

Bundle up — the grass is green today but
The gray sky is portentous and it is
Much easier to imagine a spray
Of snow descending in a bitter wind —

How much of my life have I forgotten?
How am I choosing what to remember?

Light waving
moon cycling
winter returning
remembering
forgetting.

Wheeling the receptacle of trash to
The street on Thursday morning I noticed
A light on the driveway — looking for the
Source I saw the moon brightly looming in

The sky — not appearing orange and near
The horizon but high and luminous in
In the night — cool verging into cold air
Was uncomfortable enough to rouse me

To wakefulness and I imagined the
Chinese river and mountain poets who
Renounced the contentious ways of cities
Who lived alone surrounded by mountains —

They professed to celebrate solitude
By drinking wine and savoring moonshine.

Were they savoring
bare awareness or
just dulling the pain
of loneliness?

Chinese created grasslands and rivers —
They conceived the waterfalls thundering
Into ravines — they revealed the crags of
The cloud generating mountains that brought

Sunlight and distance to life — the needles
Of a single masterful pine are
Strangely evocative and the tiny
Figure dressed in rags relying on a

Staff crossing a rickety bridge spanning —
Emptiness — are all that is left behind
Of a life — leaving me to imagine
The sinuous motion of a brush and

Wrist tracing in single lines of flowing
Ink only the essential impressions.

Someone dedicated
so much of himself to
crafting sinuous lines
of ink tracing only
the barest outlines.

A part of me always rejoices with
The sight of red and orange leaves every
Autumn — maybe because of persisting
Memories I have of dressing up in

Colorful costumes for Halloween in
Childhood — because we made the changing
Of the seasons into winter festive by
By creating a ceremony to

Cover up the withdrawal of vibrancy
And the imminence of shadowy months —
But apart from ceremony — and in
Themselves — the autumn leaves are beautiful —

The scarlet and orange and yellow leaves
Remind me beauty is temporary.

And yet beauty
reappears
reliably
spontaneously.

Not only am I — depending on the my
Mood — seeing a distorted image of
Myself and of my place within the world —
As if I were a funhouse mirror — but

I consider how my acquaintances
And my friends see themselves and their places
Within the world and I discover how
Differently strangely and opposed to my

Way of thinking they really are — then I
Ask myself are all of us — depending
On our various moods — living in one
World or are we a baffled company

Milling through a hall of funhouse mirrors
And it's a wonder we communicate.

Usually I'm better off
listening more than speaking
because listening opens
my ears and allows
the fumes to escape.

I am not burdened by the drizzling rain
Because I don't have to shovel the rain
But in a couple of weeks or even
Days the precipitation will turn to

Snow and snow on the driveways and streets is
Hazardous if not removed — the window pane
Is streaked with the rills of rain on the verge
Of freezing distorting the view of my

Cottonwood — the cottonwood has dropped a
Scattered allotment of leaves but even
A boisterous wind cannot take the leaves from
The tree because the tree isn't ready —

Isn't finished drinking the sunshine yet
Isn't prepared for its unconsciousness.

All at once the yellow
leaves come down to
brighten the grass and
rapidly they become
brittle and brown.

In summer all the leaves up and down the
Cottonwood will flutter in a breeze and
Sparkle in the sunlight and it's easy
To imagine the leaves are bells pealing

Leafy music — perhaps in the darkness
Of the night and on an overcast day
The tree is resting and sipping as much
Of the sunlight and moonlight as it can —

As every leaf is a little tongue and
Always receptive — but over a week
In autumn there comes a time when the tree
Releases its leaves and becomes dormant —

My cottonwood is harmonious with
The revolutions of the earth and sun.

All the trees
release their leaves
when the time comes in
effortless harmony.

Maybe in the future technology
Will give birth to genetically enhanced
Human beings leveraging implanted
Computer chips focusing cognition

But today I am enjoying my new
Toyota Corolla — with leather seats
And a sunroof — interfacing with my
Phone enabling me to make calls while

My hands are guiding the steering wheel — while
Receiving voice and screen directions to
My destination as I maneuver
Using satellites orbiting the earth —

But what would happen if technology
Were applied as a tool of surveillance?

Technology tracking
driving patterns
communication
likes and dislikes
even thoughts?

When the leaves are blowing in the wind in
Swirls or one by one the bareness of the
Branches and the trunks are gradually
Revealed again for another winter

And the dissipation of the leaves in
Stillwater — depending on the timing
Of the differing trees — happens over
A couple of weeks — the brightness of the

Foliage precedes a stark nakedness and
The rustling of the wind in the leaves is
Noticeably absent — I am living
Alone in a house full of memories

And the dispersal of my family
This morning came as a revelation.

Stabs of
memory
reside in
household
items.

The snow blower's electric starter is
Not working and in November it takes
Wrenching excruciating exhausting
Pulls of the starter cord to make it go

The machine was getting worse every year
And on the occasion of the first snow
Last winter my pulling was quite futile —
My swearing made no difference at all —

In February the machine will start
With a single pull but in November
It's an obstacle I dread confronting
And I'm yanking on the cord in nightmares

So this year I borrowed the use of a
Friend's pickup truck and took it for repair.

The mechanic mumbled
something about
flushing the carburetor
changing spark plugs
too much oil in the gas.

Kitcat likes the dry food the other cats
Aren't allowed because of their aliments
And I feed him alone in my bedroom —
I serve his food within a Tupperware

Container and when he's done he pounds on
The door for me to let him out — and I
Let him out and lid the container and
Put it away so he can't knock it off

The counter — as he often does just so
He can seize my attention — but today
As soon as I let him out and lidded
The container he was looking for the

Container to knock it off the counter
And he was yowling to be fed again.

I thought women were
tricky but Kitcat with
a brain the size of a
walnut is bossing
me around.

When the trees have dispersed their leaves again
When seeing through the bare branches again
Comes as a shock on a frosty morning —
Then the sunrise on the horizon is

Brilliant — as the touches of yellow and
Orange and pink spread along a distant
Line and shine in a predominately
Drab landscape — and when the sun emerges

On the horizon the light seems to rise
From the frosty grass revealing again
The subdued greens of the shrubs and pines — then
The motion of the cars reverberates

Along the streets and between the homes of
Stillwater — echoing in the quiet.

I notice the
necessity for
gloves and boots and
fabric to wrap
around my neck.

The weight of an overcast sky can be
Oppressive and ominous of coming
Burdens when the seasons turn to winter
Again when the bare branches suddenly

Take on a skeletal appearance — in
November the cold arises with a
Shock despite repeated experience —
Like being dunked into freezing water —

But I am noticing the covering
Sky in another light giving the sun
Due appreciation for persistence
And for the penetration of daylight —

Even when the snow is descending in
Overwhelming flakes the sun is present.

An overcast sky
even the cascading
snowflakes are
suffused and glowing
with sunlight.

His ears are enormous extending out
From his head and appearing sensitive
And capable of absorbing whispers —
His nose and nostrils are exorbitant

His chin and teeth are prominent — and with
The large dark pools of his eyes he gazes
About steadily and peacefully and then
Suddenly he can become excited —

He is sloped-shouldered and elongated
And his neck and legs are especially
Exaggerated in length and when he
Moves he ambles and lopes in swinging strides

Rhythmically and lackadaisically
And yet he covers the ground quite quickly.

The
muscular
tongue
can
grab
leaves
but
why
does
the
giraffe
have
two
horns?

There are so many details hanging in
The air without worthy explanation
And I have often lain awake at night
Wondering why do the giraffes have tails

Because in proportion to their bodies
This little protuberance wouldn't serve
As much protection as a fly swatter
Except the to sensitive puckering

Directly under the tail — and the tuft
Would be quite unnecessary for that —
Perhaps in the compilation of the
Organism the flicking or swishing

Instrument is useful for expression
Or maybe it's only an afterthought?

A
quizzical
swish
or
a
petulant
flick
could
be
quite
communicative.

If lawyers had tails they would exercise
Caution and discipline in the courtroom
Not to flicker nervously about but
To swish with confidence and rectitude

When upon their hind legs questioning a
Witness or presenting evidence — and
They would eliminate superfluous
Gesturing including the wayward tips

Practicing a curl of dignity or
An upright pose of sobriety while
Leaving for the closing arguments the
Dramatically vigorous sweep and snap

Or imagine the declamatory
Righteousness of unwavering tautness.

Out of
court
lawyers
with tails
could
afford
to
be
limp
and
list-
less.

The days between my disposal of the
Cottonwood leaves and blizzards are blissful
Because I don't have to do anything
Outside and the wind may howl in the trees

And the temperature may plummet but
I'm prepared with winter fleeces mittens
Boots and berets — and the warmest blankets —
The furnace is humming the curtains are

Drawn against the early evening darkness
And the car is safe within the garage —
Preparing for snow is a ritual
Repeated year after year becoming

A somber celebration once the work
Is finished harvesting satisfaction.

On some years the ground
stays bare of snow until
Christmas and I'm fooled
thinking this will be
an easy winter.

When remembering previous winters
It is easy to be casual in
Conversation recalling a storm in
March or a snowfall in November or

The few days in January when we
Seemed to be having a surprising spring
Followed of course by a blasting of cold
And a battering of blizzards with the

Snow accumulating in piles along
Streets and driveways higher than me because
I was freezing my fingers pushing a
Snow blower and scraping with a shovel —

Winter in Minnesota becomes a
Nonsensical trudging in the tundra.

I am a
survivor with
post traumatic
February
disorder.

The apple trees
and lilac bushes
bloom together in spring
and hold their leaves
past the first snowfall.

— *Tekkan*

www.ingramcontent.com/pod-product-compliance
Lightning Source LLC
Chambersburg PA
CBHW042118100526
44587CB00025B/4102